For more information, please contact by email johanna@hurmerinta.com

Author: Johanna Hurmerinta.
Designer and photographer: Johanna Hurmerinta.
Publisher: Johanna Hurmerinta.
Distributor: IngramSpark. ISBN paperback: 978-952-94-5541-6

A coral reef
is a colony of small and big
corals in the sea.
The color of corals can be white,
pink, purple, red,
green, brown and yellow.

The Clownfish live in a
symbiotic relationship
with sea anemones.
This means the fish benefit from
living with the sea anemone,
and the sea anemone benefits
from the presence
of the clownfish.

All other fish get stung by the tentacles of the anemone.

The sea turtles
are slow swimmers.
They cannot breathe underwater.
They can swim for 5 hours
without breathing.
Then they must swim
to the surface for air.

Despite their name,
jellyfish are not really fish.
They are invertebrates. That means
they do not have a backbone.
Some jellyfish
can even glow in the dark!

Jellyfish have been around
for over 500 million years!

Stingrays are found in
shallow coastal waters.
They spend most of their time
inactive, partially buried
in the sand.
Stingrays eat
clams, shrimp and mussels.

The Exquisite Butterflyfish
are so beautiful.
They have black stripes across their
eyes and eye-like spots
on the body.
These serve to confuse the
predators and allow the fish
to escape on time.

The Royal Angelfish
is one of the most colorful fish
on the coral reef.
With its bright colors
it is a very beautiful fish.
This fish can live up to 15 years.

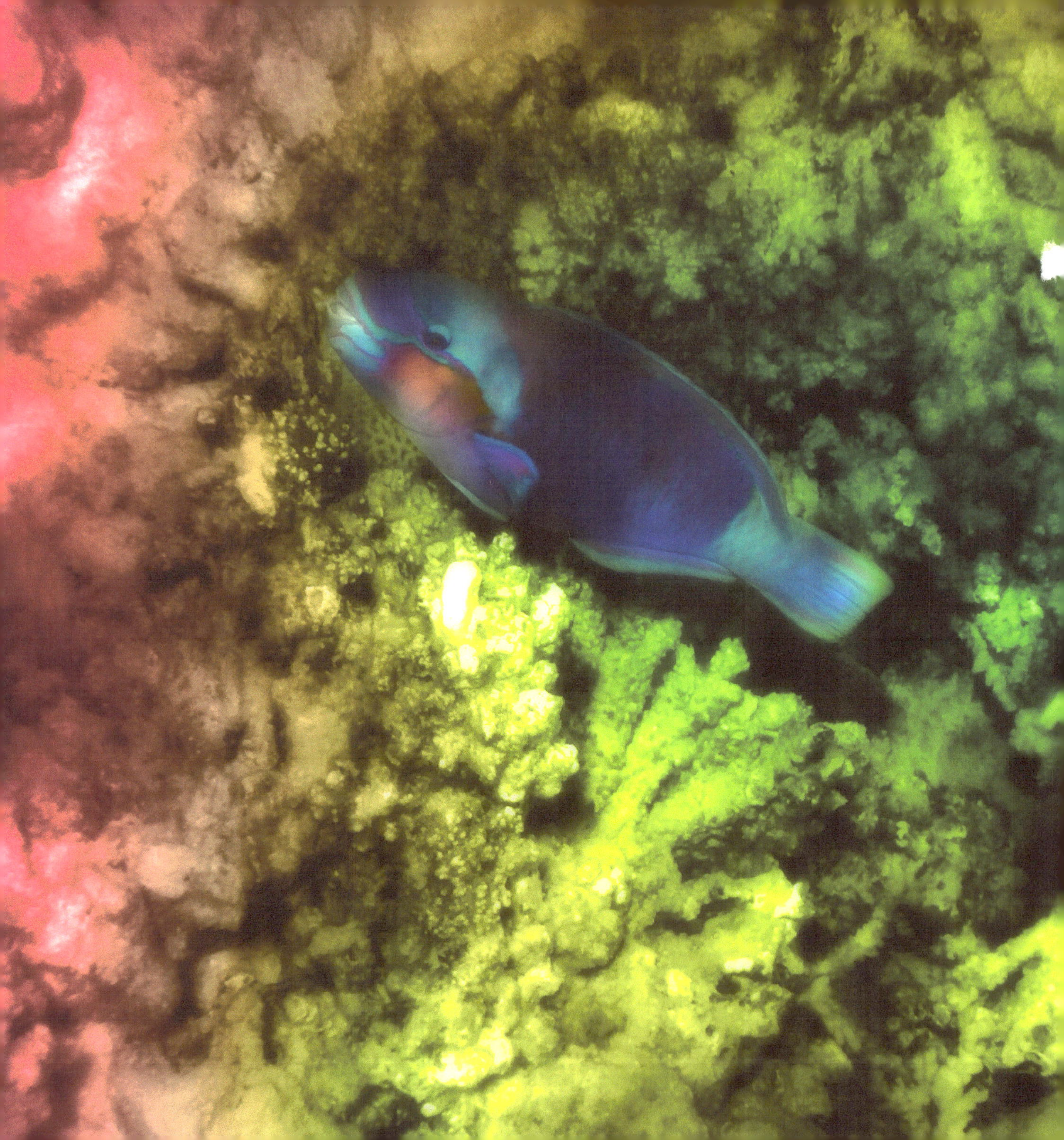

The Daisy Parrotfish is
one of the most widespread
parrotfish species.

There are 95 species
of parrotfish in the world.

This fish is found on the
Red Sea coral reefs.
It is the Arabian Picassofish.

It needs a varied diet of food
including squid, clams and hard
shelled shrimp to help wear down
its ever growing teeth.

The Sailfin Tang has a large
top fin which it opens like a sail
when it feels threatened.
It wants to look bigger and
make the enemy swim away.

The Silverspot Squirrelfish
is a red fish with a touch of
silver color.
It is a nocturnal fish.
This means it is most
active during the night.

The Yellowstripe Goatfish
feel safer in a group.

Fish evolved to swim in schools to
better protect themselves
from predators.

We feel safer being close together.

ABOUT THE AUTHOR

Hi. My name is Johanna Hurmerinta. I live in Finland, Europe.

I love to photograph underwater. The coral reefs are so beautiful. I have photographed in the Red Sea in Africa during many years.

I created this picture book so young children and their parents or grandparents can enjoy wonderful and magical moments in the underwater world.

I have also written and designed a picture book for children age 5-9 years. The name of the book is THE ADVENTURES OF THE PICASSOFISH. This book can be ordered from many online bookstores, for example from Amazon US, UK, CA or DE, and from Barnes & Noble in the US.

www.ingramcontent.com/pod-product-compliance
Ingram Content Group UK Ltd.
Pitfield, Milton Keynes, MK11 3LW, UK
UKHW060110300726
14090UKWH00002B/116
* 9 7 8 9 5 2 9 4 5 5 4 1 6 *